P9-BIN-066

New Testament

Adventure BIBLE StoryBook

WRITTEN BY
Catherine DeVries

ILLUSTRATED BY
Jim Madsen

This book belongs to:

_____

ZONDERkidz

ZONDERVAN.com/
AUTHORTRACKER
follow your favorite authors

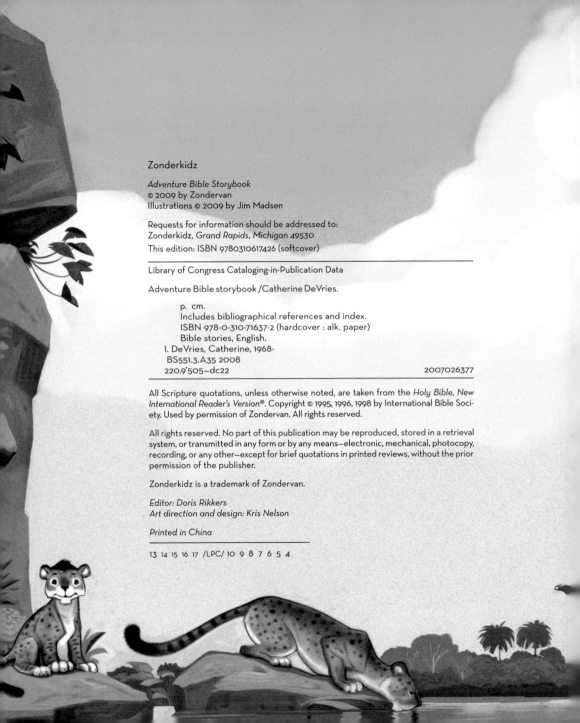

Zonderkidz

Adventure Bible Storybook
© 2009 by Zondervan
Illustrations © 2009 by Jim Madsen

Requests for information should be addressed to:
Zonderkidz, *Grand Rapids, Michigan 49530*
This edition: ISBN 9780310617426 (softcover)

Library of Congress Cataloging-in-Publication Data

Adventure Bible storybook /Catherine DeVries.

    p. cm.
    Includes bibliographical references and index.
    ISBN 978-0-310-71637-2 (hardcover : alk. paper)
    Bible stories, English.
  I. DeVries, Catherine, 1968-
  BS551.3.A35 2008
  220.9'505—dc22   2007026377

All Scripture quotations, unless otherwise noted, are taken from the *Holy Bible, New International Reader's Version*®. Copyright © 1995, 1996, 1998 by International Bible Society. Used by permission of Zondervan. All rights reserved.

All rights reserved. No part of this publication may be reproduced, stored in a retrieval system, or transmitted in any form or by any means—electronic, mechanical, photocopy, recording, or any other—except for brief quotations in printed reviews, without the prior permission of the publisher.

Zonderkidz is a trademark of Zondervan.

Editor: Doris Rikkers
Art direction and design: Kris Nelson

Printed in China

---

13 14 15 16 17 /LPC/ 10 9 8 7 6 5 4

To you, Brad—the love of my life—
and to our children, Bryce, Breia, and Brent.
May our home always be filled with laughter,
good books, and especially God's love.
—Catherine

To my mom and dad,
who encouraged me to
color within the lines
but forgave me when I didn't.
— Jim

Table of Contents

Earth Bound

Luke 2:1 – 7

The world was silent. And most everyone was fast asleep. What seemed like a normal night, with the moon and the stars shining brightly overhead, would become a night like no other.

A woman rode a donkey into Bethlehem. Her tummy was huge. Very soon she would give birth to her baby. Joseph and Mary went to every inn to see if there was any room for them to stay. But at all the doors, the people just shook their heads no. Then a door opened. A man peered out and noticed Mary.

"Looks like she needs a place to rest," he said. "You can stay in my stable out back. It's not much, but at least it's warm and dry."

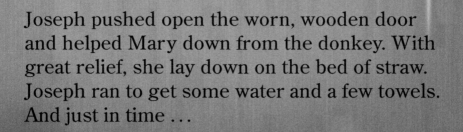

Joseph pushed open the worn, wooden door and helped Mary down from the donkey. With great relief, she lay down on the bed of straw. Joseph ran to get some water and a few towels. And just in time ...

Mary's son was born. His cries in the night echoed through the empty streets of Bethlehem.

Mary looked down at her precious baby boy. "Hello, Jesus," she whispered. She laid him down and snuggled close.

God had come to earth as a little baby. He would someday save the world.

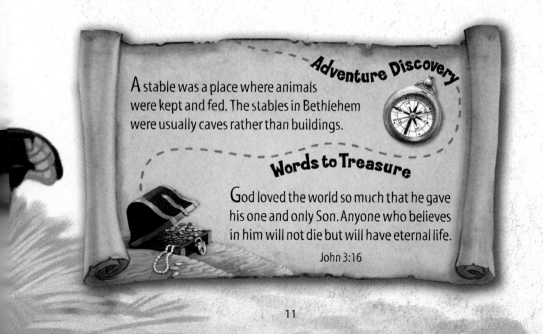

Adventure Discovery

A stable was a place where animals were kept and fed. The stables in Bethlehem were usually caves rather than buildings.

Words to Treasure

God loved the world so much that he gave his one and only Son. Anyone who believes in him will not die but will have eternal life.

John 3:16

Angels Tell the Shepherds

Luke 2:8 – 20

That same evening outside the city, shepherds gathered around a campfire and relaxed after a hard day's work in the open fields.

From out of nowhere, an angel appeared with a very important announcement: "Christ the Savior is born. Go and find him."

The shepherds looked up and heard singing. Hundreds of angels joined together in a huge choir. They sang, "May glory be given to God in the highest heaven! And may peace be given to those he is pleased with on earth!"

The shepherds forgot about the campfire and their hard day. They were mesmerized by the singing. They had never seen such sights and sounds as these.

When the angels disappeared, the shepherds hurried to the nearby town of Bethlehem.

They found baby Jesus and praised God. The Savior of the world had come!

Adventure Discovery

The Bible gives us the names of only two angels: Gabriel and Michael. But we do not know if they were in the choir of angels who sang when Jesus was born.

Words to Treasure

"Today in the town of David a Savior has been born to you. He is Christ the Lord."

Luke 2:11

Gifts from the Wise Men

Matthew 2:1 – 12

A brilliant star shone in the dark night sky. The wise men looked at each other. They knew what this meant. A king was born!

The men packed their bags and loaded their camels for the trip. It was going to take some time. But they knew the star would lead them to the new king. So they followed it.

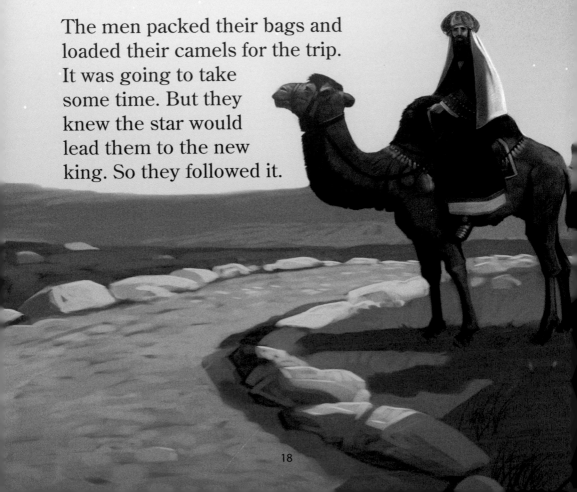

19

The men stopped at King Herod's palace in Jerusalem. "Where is the king of the Jews who has been born?" they asked.

King Herod was not happy because he did not want another king in his kingdom. He asked the priests and teachers of the law if they knew where this king was.

"The prophet said he would come to Bethlehem," they told King Herod.

The king told the wise men, "Look for the baby in Bethlehem and tell me where you find him."

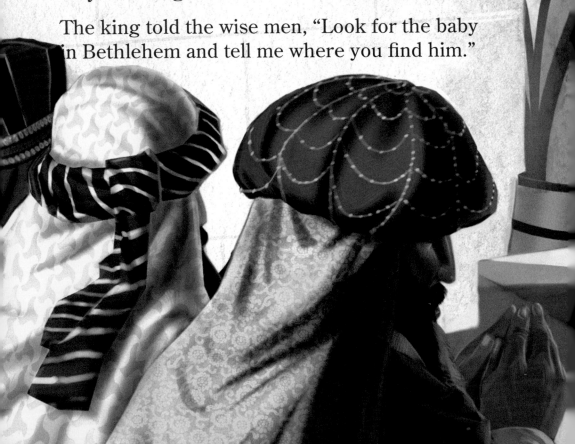

The wise men continued to follow the star, and it led them to a little house. This was it!

A woman opened the door. And a little toddler peeked out from behind her skirt. The wise men entered, each with a present. They put their gifts at the feet of young Jesus — gold and rich spices. Gifts fit for a king. They had found the Son of God.

The wise men were warned in a dream not to go back to King Herod. So they went home without telling the king where Jesus was.

Adventure Discovery

Jesus was about two years old when the wise men came to visit him.

Words to Treasure

"Where is the child who has been born to be king of the Jews? When we were in the east, we saw his star. Now we have come to worship him."

Matthew 2:2

Lost?

Luke 2:41 – 52

Every year Jesus and his family traveled from their home in Nazareth to Jerusalem for the Passover celebration. But this year, on their way home, the festive feeling of the holiday disappeared.

Jesus, who was now twelve years old, was missing. Without wasting another minute, Mary and Joseph hurried back to the city to find their son. But no one had seen him. No one knew where he was.

After three days of searching and worry, Mary rested on a bench outside the temple.

Wait. What was that? Mary knew that voice. It was Jesus! She ran through the entrance of the temple and found him talking with the church leaders. He listened to their questions and gave the answers. The leaders were amazed by his understanding.

Mary ran to Jesus and hugged him. "Where have you been?" she asked. "We were so worried!"

Jesus replied, "Didn't you know I had to be in my Father's house?"

Mary looked at her calm son. She didn't understand everything, but she knew Jesus was special. Someday he would save the world. But right then, she just kissed his forehead and said, "I love you, Jesus." She took his hand, joined Joseph, and headed back to Nazareth, where Jesus learned how to be a carpenter until his ministry began.

Adventure Discovery

A carpenter is someone who builds things out of wood, like chairs and houses.

Words to Treasure

Jesus became wiser and stronger. He also became more and more pleasing to God and to people.

Luke 2:52

Jesus Is Baptized

Matthew 3:13 – 17

The water shimmered and sparkled in the sunlight as the people waded in. John stood in the middle of the river, ready to baptize whoever came to him. When he looked up, he recognized his cousin Jesus.

John shook his head. He said, "I need to be baptized by *you*, Jesus. So why do you come to me?"

"It is right for us to do this," Jesus replied. "It carries out God's holy plan."

So John baptized Jesus, dunking him completely under water, just like the others.

As soon as Jesus came out of the water, the skies opened up.

Jesus saw the Spirit of God coming down on him like a dove.

A voice from heaven said, "This is my Son, and I love him. I am very pleased with him."

Jesus left the river and went into the desert to fast and to pray for forty days.

Adventure Discovery

People are still baptized today.
Some are baptized when they are babies.
Others are baptized when they are older.

Words to Treasure

"This is my Son, and I love him.
I am very pleased with him."

Matthew 3:17

The Devil Tempts Jesus

Matthew 4:1 – 11

The hot sun beat down on the desert—the cactus, the lizards, the sand. Jesus wiped the sweat from his forehead as he prayed. It had been more than one month since Jesus had eaten anything.

Satan knew Jesus was hungry, and he hoped Jesus would be weak. Maybe this would be a good time to trick Jesus into sinning, he thought. So the Devil said to Jesus, "If you are the Son of God, tell these stones to become bread."

Jesus replied, "'Man doesn't live only on bread. He also lives on every word that comes from the mouth of the Lord'" (Deuteronomy 8:3). Jesus had passed the first test.

Then Jesus stood at the top of the temple. The Devil said, "If you are the Son of God, throw yourself down. It is written, 'The Lord will command his angels to take good care of you.'"

Jesus answered, "It is also written, 'Don't put the Lord your God to the test'" (Deuteronomy 6:16). Jesus had passed the second test.

Then Jesus stood on a very high mountain. The Devil showed him all the kingdoms of the world and their glory. "If you bow down and worship me," Satan said, "I will give you all of this."

Jesus said, "Get away from me, Satan! It is written, 'Worship the Lord your God. He is the only one you should serve'" (Deuteronomy 6:13). Jesus had passed the third test.

The Devil could not trick Jesus. So the Devil left. And angels came and took care of Jesus.

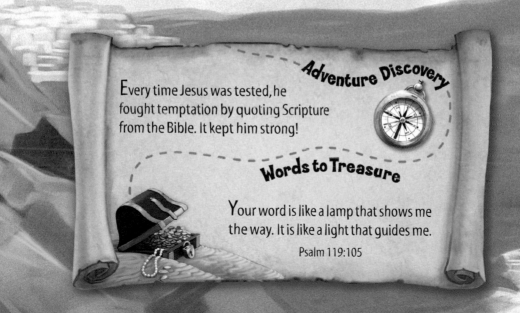

Adventure Discovery

Every time Jesus was tested, he fought temptation by quoting Scripture from the Bible. It kept him strong!

Words to Treasure

Your word is like a lamp that shows me the way. It is like a light that guides me.

Psalm 119:105

Calling the Disciples

Matthew 4:18 – 22

The waves gently rolled onto the beach as Jesus walked along the shore. He scanned the horizon and saw what he was looking for. Two boats bobbed on the waves in the distance with fish nets drifting in the water.

Jesus waved to the fishermen in the boats. "Come. Follow me!" he called.

Jesus' words captured their attention. The fishermen wanted to find out who this person was. When they rowed closer to shore, Jesus said, "I will make you fishers of people."

Now they were really interested. They left their boats and fish nets behind and went with Jesus.

They never imagined they were beginning the biggest adventure of their lives—being disciples of Jesus!

Adventure Discovery

Fishing was a common occupation in Jesus' time. Fishermen on the Sea of Galilee caught different kinds of fish — carp, sardines, and tilapia.

Words to Treasure

"Come. Follow me," Jesus said.

Matthew 4:19

Through the Roof

Mark 2:1 – 12

What was all the commotion? Dozens and
dozens of people passed the man as they
hurried to a nearby house. They kicked up dust
so thick the man started to cough. His cough
shook his entire body, causing his lame leg to
slip off his mat. He pulled it back with his good
arm. Then he lay back down, exhausted.

Another group of people approached—friends of the man. Each one took a corner of his mat. They lifted him up and carried him down the street. One of his friends grinned and said, "We're going to see Jesus, and we're taking you with us."

Crowds of people surrounded the house where Jesus was. So the four friends went up the stairs of the house to the flat roof. Nothing was going to stop them from getting their friend to Jesus.

In a matter of minutes, the man was lowered through a hole in the roof right in front of Jesus.

Jesus looked at the man. Then he looked up at the roof and saw the four friends peering in. Jesus saw their faith. He turned to the man on the mat and said, "Your sins are forgiven. Get up. Take your mat and go home."

The man was astonished. He got up and walked outside where his friends were waiting. They ran down the street together, celebrating this amazing thing Jesus had done!

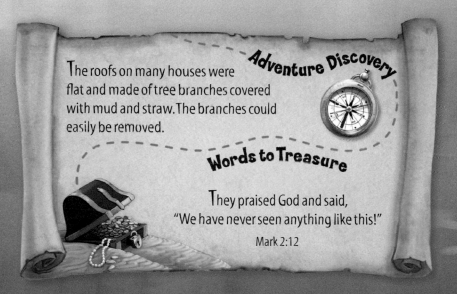

Adventure Discovery

The roofs on many houses were flat and made of tree branches covered with mud and straw. The branches could easily be removed.

Words to Treasure

They praised God and said, "We have never seen anything like this!"

Mark 2:12

Do Not Worry

Matthew 6:25 – 34

Crowds of people followed Jesus. They wanted to hear him teach. So he went up on a mountainside and sat down. His disciples were there too.

Jesus said to the crowd, "I tell you, do not worry. Don't worry about your life and what you will eat or drink. And don't worry about your body and what you will wear. Isn't there more to life than eating? Aren't there more important things for the body than clothes?

"Look at the birds of the air," said Jesus, pointing to the sky. "They don't plant or gather crops. They don't put away crops in storerooms. But your Father who is in heaven feeds them. Aren't you worth much more than they are?"

Beautiful flowers dotted the hillside. Their delicate petals fluttered in the wind. And they smelled as sweet as perfume.

"And why do you worry about clothes?" said Jesus. "See how the wildflowers grow. They don't work or make clothing."

Then Jesus compared the flowers to King Solomon, Israel's richest king. "Not even Solomon in all of his glory was dressed like one of those flowers," he said. If God dresses the grass of the field so beautifully, won't he dress us even better?

It doesn't help to worry. It won't add "even one hour" of time to our lives. God knows we need food and clothes. And he will give them to us, explained Jesus.

"Put God's kingdom first," said Jesus. "Do what he wants you to do. Then all of those things will also be given to you."

Adventure Discovery

To put "God's kingdom first" means
to choose things that would please
God above everything else.

Words to Treasure

"I tell you, do not worry."

Matthew 6:25

Treasure!

Matthew 13:44–45

The day was coming to a close, with the setting sun low in the sky. But the man didn't notice because he was so determined to find what he was looking for. He had sold everything to buy this field because he knew it held something special.

Dig, throw, dig, throw. His back ached and his hands throbbed, but he pressed on. *Clank!* went his shovel. "It must be a rock," sighed the man. He kept working. Soon he realized that this was no rock. This was what he had been searching for … *treasure!*

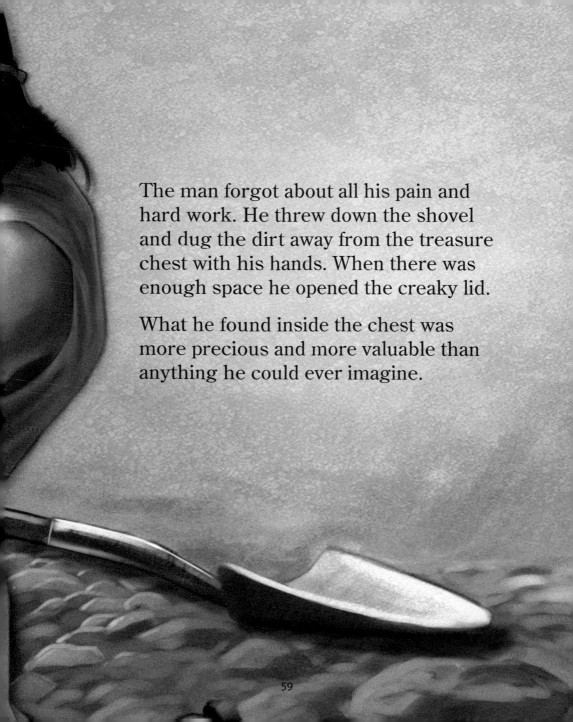

The man forgot about all his pain and hard work. He threw down the shovel and dug the dirt away from the treasure chest with his hands. When there was enough space he opened the creaky lid.

What he found inside the chest was more precious and more valuable than anything he could ever imagine.

Jesus taught the people many things about the kingdom of heaven so they could understand what it was like. He told them this story about finding treasure: "The kingdom of heaven is like treasure that was hidden in a field. When a man found it, he hid it again. He was very happy. So he went and sold everything he had. And he bought that field."

Jesus said that we should search for God like the man searched for the treasure. We need to keep at it, keep pressing on, keep digging deeper to know him, love him, and follow him.

Adventure Discovery

People in ancient times did not have banks. They buried their treasures and money in a field. Sometimes the treasure would not be found for many years.

Words to Treasure

"The kingdom of heaven is like treasure that was hidden in a field."

Matthew 13:44

Stormy Night

Matthew 8:23 – 27

The calm night of sailing across the Sea of Galilee had turned into a stormy disaster. The disciples controlled the boat as best they could, but water was pouring in and they were afraid.

They called out, "Jesus, save us!"

Jesus rubbed his eyes. Just moments ago he had been sleeping in the boat, unaware of the change in the weather.

Frightened, the disciples clung with all their might to the sides of the boat. But not Jesus. He stood up and simply said to the storm, "Be still!"

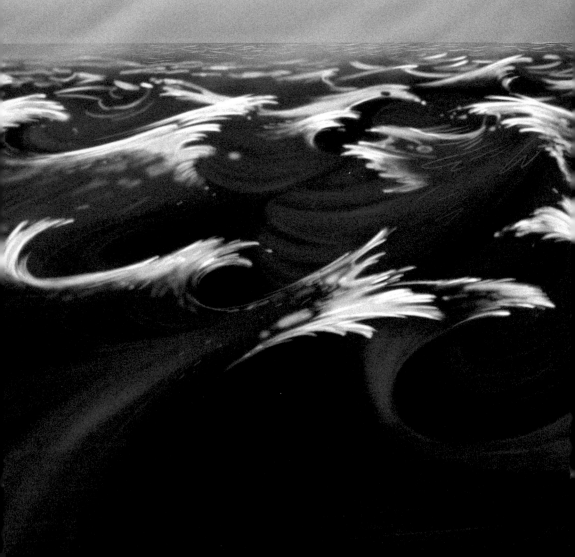

The storm stopped, just like that. The blowing wind and the powerful waves turned to calm with two words from the Son of God.

The disciples turned to each other in relief and amazement. "What kind of man is this? Even the winds and the waves obey him!"

They had never experienced anything like this. And they would never forget.

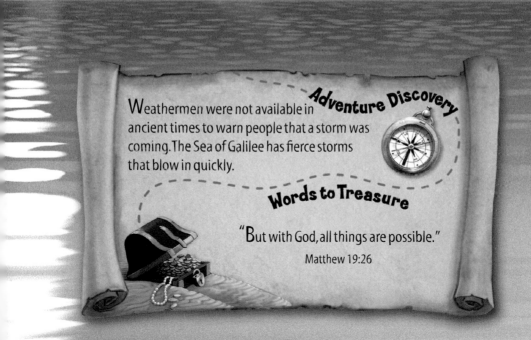

Adventure Discovery

Weathermen were not available in ancient times to warn people that a storm was coming. The Sea of Galilee has fierce storms that blow in quickly.

Words to Treasure

"But with God, all things are possible."

Matthew 19:26

Jesus Heals a Woman

Luke 8:43 – 48

Just a few steps more and she would be in front of Jesus. But too many people stood in the way, and she couldn't push through the crowd. She leaned hard on her cane, and her shoulders slumped. For a moment she thought about turning around and going home.

No! she told herself. Do not give up. Here is
Jesus. He is your only hope. The woman reached
through the crowd of people, stretching, her hand
shaking. Finally she touched his cloak.

Immediately she felt a surge of power go through her. And heal her.

Jesus turned around and asked, "Who touched me?"

The woman fell at his feet and said, "I did. I touched you."

"Good woman," he said, eyes filled with love and tenderness. "Please, get up. Your faith has healed you."

This man Jesus was amazing! He had changed her life. She dropped her cane and walked tall. Today was a new day. All because of Jesus. She was healed!

Adventure Discovery

This very sick woman had been bleeding for twelve years.

Words to Treasure

He said to her, "Dear woman, your faith has healed you. Go in peace. You are free from your suffering."

Mark 5:34

Run for Her Life

Luke 8:40 – 55

Just a little bit farther, the man told himself. His heart was pounding so hard he was afraid it would burst. But all he could think about was his little girl. She was so sick and needed help right away. Just when he felt like he couldn't go any farther, he saw a crowd up ahead.

Jesus turned around as the man approached. "Jesus," the man called out. "Jesus, please help. My daughter is very sick," he said as he bent down to catch his breath.

Just then a messenger came up to the crowd and pulled the man aside. He did not have good news. The little girl had died. Jesus put his hand on the man's shoulder and said, "It's not too late. Your daughter will be healed. Just believe."

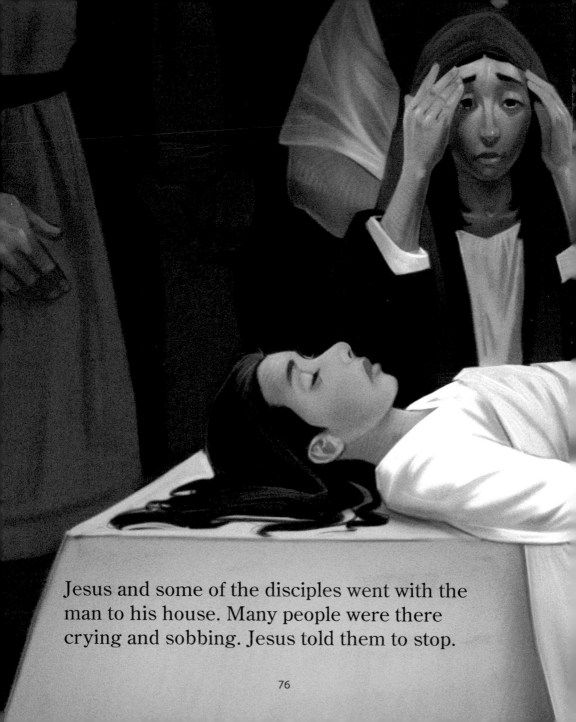

Jesus and some of the disciples went with the man to his house. Many people were there crying and sobbing. Jesus told them to stop.

He went to the girl, along with her mom and dad. As she lay very still on her bed, Jesus took her hand. "My child, get up!" he said.

The girl opened her eyes and looked around.
She was alive again!

Her dad scooped her up in his arms. He kissed her as happy tears streamed down his face.

Jesus had done the impossible. He had brought the little girl back to life!

Adventure Discovery

The little girl's father was the ruler of the synagogue. He would lead the service, select people to help, and make sure that everyone followed the rules.

Words to Treasure

"Don't be afraid. Just believe. She will be healed."

Luke 8:50

Jesus Heals a Blind Man

John 9:1 – 7

As Jesus walked down the road, he noticed a
blind man. The man had been blind since he
was born. The man had never seen the faces of
his mother and father. He had never seen trees
or grass or flowers. He had never seen the sun,
moon, and stars. His eyes just didn't work.

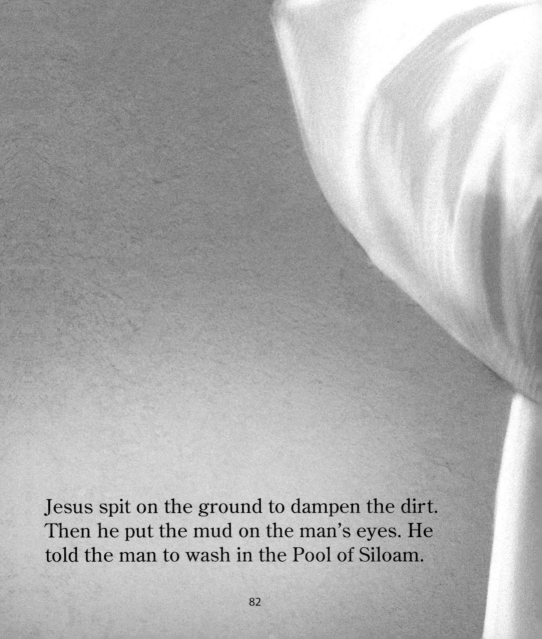

Jesus spit on the ground to dampen the dirt. Then he put the mud on the man's eyes. He told the man to wash in the Pool of Siloam.

So the man did as Jesus said. As the water washed away the mud, something began to happen. Light began to filter through the darkness. Slowly the man opened his eyes. He looked around in amazement at the trees and flowers, people and animals. How wonderful to go home and finally see the faces of his parents. How surprised and thankful to Jesus they all must have been!

Adventure Discovery

The Pool of Siloam was cut out of rocks. The water in it was considered sacred. The pool is still in Jerusalem today.

Words to Treasure

"I am the light of the world."

John 9:5

The Lost Son

Luke 15:11 – 24

What a very unusual place to find someone. There, in a muddy field surrounded by pigs, sat a filthy man. His torn clothes and tangled hair smelled like the dirty animals.

His stomach ached with hunger. He hadn't eaten in days. Even the pig slop looked good to him. He wondered, How had life come to this?

The man remembered when he had been back
home with his father and his brother. There
had always been food on the table. He had
never been hungry. He had always worn nice
clothes, and he knew his father loved him. But
still he had been determined to leave home.

He had wanted to see other places, so he had boldly demanded that his father give him his inheritance money.

At first everything turned out better than he imagined. His bag of money overflowed, and he made a lot of friends. He bought them meals and drinks and even fancy hats and sparkly rings! But as soon as his money ran out, his friends did too. Not one person stayed with him.

So the man left the city and found the best job he could, feeding pigs at a farm. And there he sat in the mud with the smelly animals.

A thought struck him. My father has plenty of servants working for him who are treated well and have good food to eat. I know I've done many bad things, but maybe my father will forgive me and let me be one of his servants.

The man got up from the pigpen and walked home. Before he even reached his house, he saw someone running down the road toward him. It was his father!

They hugged for a long time, and tears streamed down their faces. The father was so glad to see that his son had come home. He not only welcomed his son back, he dressed him with the best robe and celebrated with a huge party!

When we do something wrong, Jesus forgives us with this same kind of love.

Adventure Discovery

Feeding pigs was the worst kind of work for a Jewish person. They viewed pigs as "unclean" animals and tried to have nothing to do with them.

Words to Treasure

"While the son was still a long way off, his father saw him. He was filled with tender love for his son. He ran to him. He threw his arms around him and kissed him."

Luke 15:20

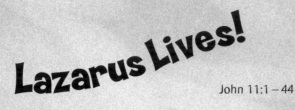

Lazarus Lives!

John 11:1 – 44

Jesus stood at the entrance of the tomb and called, "Come out!"

Like an old scary movie, a mummy walked out of the tomb, its cloth bandages starting to unravel.

Mary and Martha couldn't believe it. Four days earlier their brother had died, and they had placed him in this tomb. Now someone was walking out! Surely this couldn't be real.

The sisters held their breath. The bandages fell off. It was …

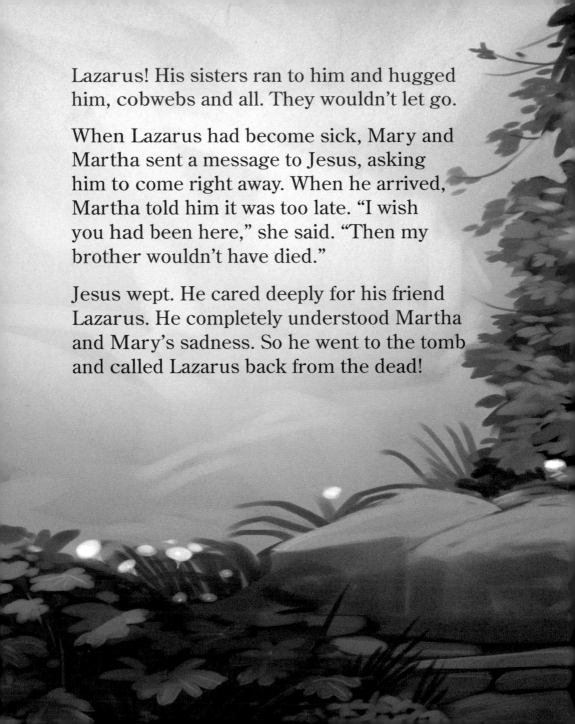

Lazarus! His sisters ran to him and hugged him, cobwebs and all. They wouldn't let go.

When Lazarus had become sick, Mary and Martha sent a message to Jesus, asking him to come right away. When he arrived, Martha told him it was too late. "I wish you had been here," she said. "Then my brother wouldn't have died."

Jesus wept. He cared deeply for his friend Lazarus. He completely understood Martha and Mary's sadness. So he went to the tomb and called Lazarus back from the dead!

That night, Jesus sat around the dinner table
with Mary, Martha, and Lazarus. They
treasured every minute and were so happy to
be together again.

Jesus has feelings just like we do. When we are sad, he is sad. He understands our pain and he cares about us.

Words to Treasure

Jesus sobbed.

John 11:35

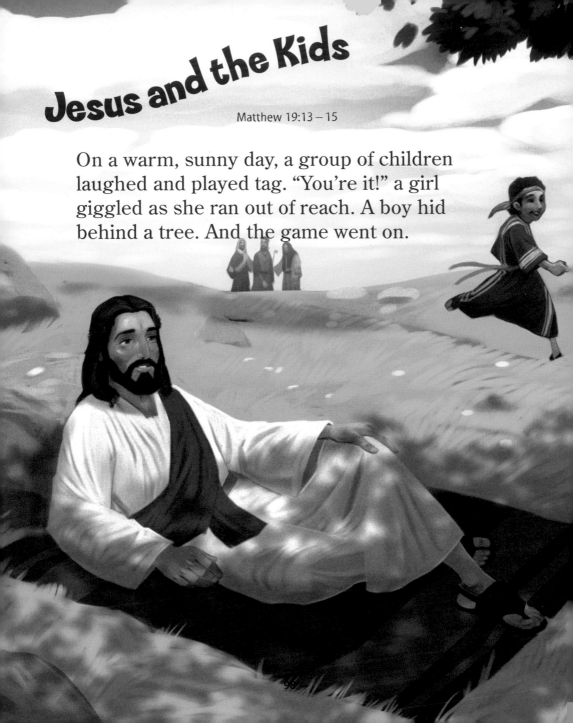

Jesus and the Kids

Matthew 19:13 – 15

On a warm, sunny day, a group of children laughed and played tag. "You're it!" a girl giggled as she ran out of reach. A boy hid behind a tree. And the game went on.

Jesus smiled at their gentle hearts, tender spirits, and fearless wonder. Oh, how he loved children. Not just these children but all the children in the whole world.

Just then their mothers called out, "Come here! Let's talk to Jesus and ask him to pray for you."

But the disciples stood in their way. "Don't bother Jesus. He's too busy," they said.

Jesus didn't agree. "Let the children come to me," he called out to the disciples. "Do not keep them away."

The children joyfully ran to Jesus, laughing and giggling.

He lifted them onto his lap and smiled at them. He laughed with them and gave them hugs.

Adventure Discovery

What a friend we have in Jesus!

Words to Treasure

Jesus said, "Let the little children come to me. Don't keep them away. The kingdom of heaven belongs to people like them."

Matthew 19:14

In the Tree Tops

Luke 19:1 – 10

Wow, what a view! The town of Jericho looked so much smaller from up in the tree. For once in his life, Zacchaeus felt like a giant. He could see his house in the distance and the road leading to it. He could see the crowd of people in the streets. And finally, at last, he could see Jesus.

A squirrel scolded Zacchaeus where he sat in the tree. He swished it away because he was trying to listen to Jesus.

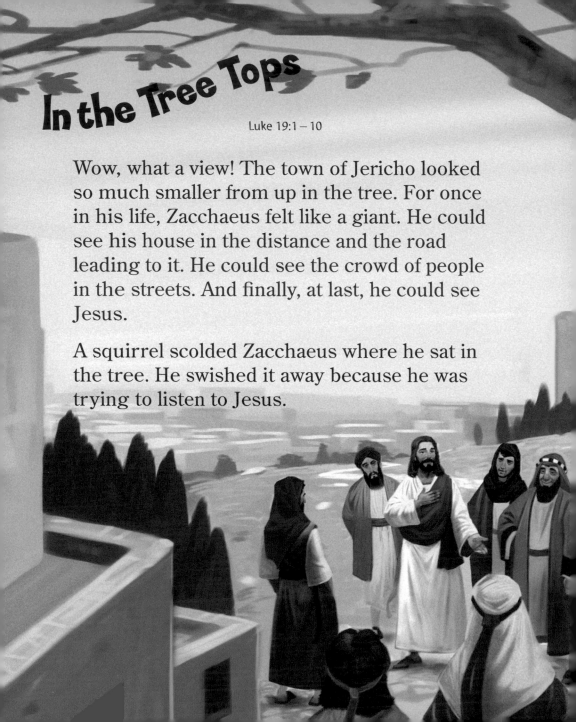

As Zacchaeus sat quietly, Jesus looked up into the tree. In front of the crowd of people, Jesus called his name. "Zacchaeus, come down from that tree. I'm going to your house today," he said.

Zacchaeus scrambled down the branches and trunk. As he scurried through the crowd, the people booed at the short man. It was no secret that Zacchaeus was a tax collector and had cheated many of his neighbors out of money.

But Jesus didn't boo. Instead, he smiled and motioned for Zacchaeus to walk with him. Soon they reached Zacchaeus' house and went inside.

By the end of their time together, Zacchaeus' life was changed. He promised Jesus he would stop his bad ways and pay people back four times the amount of money he had stolen from them.

As Zacchaeus waved good-bye, he felt thankful for Jesus' visit. He took out his money and started counting it — to see how much he needed to return. Through his window he could see the big tree … and he grinned.

Adventure Discovery

Tax collectors collected money from the people for the government. But many tax collectors took more money than was needed, so they could keep some for themselves.

Words to Treasure

Put up with each other. Forgive the things you are holding against one another. Forgive, just as the Lord forgave you.

Colossians 3:13

A Friendship Is Lost

John 13:1 – 30

The disciples gathered together with Jesus to eat supper. Their feet were dusty from the dirt roads. Jesus bent down and washed their feet, surprising each person there. The disciples didn't understand. Why would Jesus make himself their servant? But Jesus was teaching them an important lesson: they needed to be servants to others.

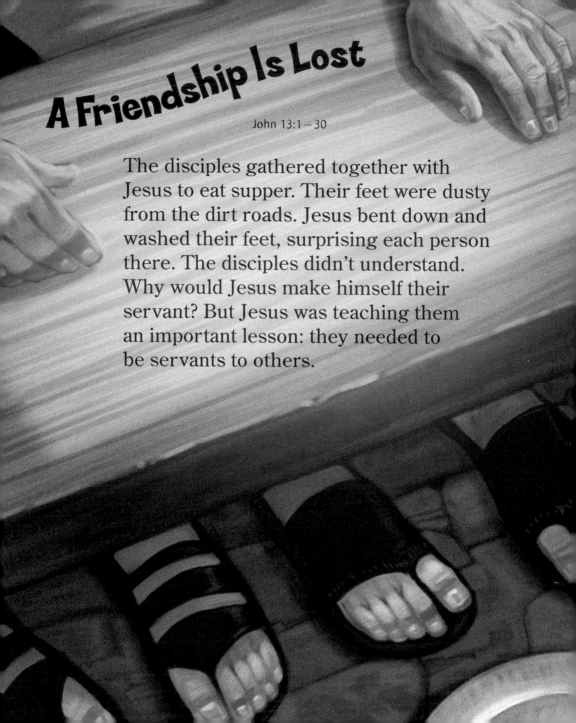

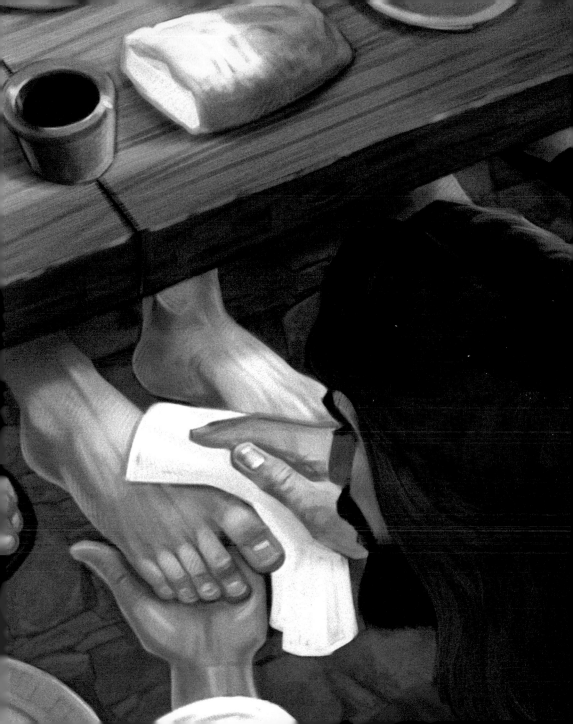

As the sun was setting, the disciples sat at the table. Jesus locked eyes with Judas. Then he turned to the rest of them. Jesus broke the bread on his plate and said, "This is my body, given for you." Then he poured wine into his cup and said, "This is my blood, shed for you."

As they finished supper, Jesus motioned for them to pay attention to him. "One of you will betray me this very night," said Jesus. The disciples looked at each other in disbelief.

"Surely, it isn't me?" one person said. "Jesus, is it me?" asked another. In the midst of the questions, Jesus again locked eyes with Judas.

Then Judas slipped out the back door into the night.

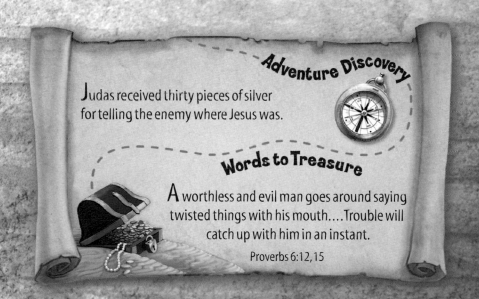

Adventure Discovery

Judas received thirty pieces of silver for telling the enemy where Jesus was.

Words to Treasure

A worthless and evil man goes around saying twisted things with his mouth....Trouble will catch up with him in an instant.

Proverbs 6:12, 15

Jesus Is Captured

Matthew 26:36 – 46

After the disciples were finished eating supper, a few of them walked with Jesus to a garden called Gethsemane. This was one of Jesus' favorite places to pray. "Stay. Sit here while I go over there to pray," he said to them.

Jesus walked over to a group of trees, knelt on the ground, and began to pray to God, his Father.

Jesus knew that his time on earth was coming to an end. He thought about all the people he had met and how much he loved them.

Jesus prayed, "Father, take this suffering from me. But if it is your will, then I will accept that too."

His body shook. Sweat poured down his face as he prayed about the trouble that was coming.

Jesus got up and walked back to the disciples. They were sleeping. Jesus sighed. He would have to face his suffering alone.

Then he saw torches coming in the distance.

Adventure Discovery

The garden of Gethsemane is located on a hill called the Mount of Olives. The garden had many olive trees in it when Jesus was alive.

Words to Treasure

"My Father, if it is possible, take this cup of suffering away from me. But let what you want be done, not what I want."

Matthew 26:39

Love Wins

Matthew 26:47 – 49; John 19:17 – 18

The flickering torches got closer and closer to where Jesus was in the garden of Gethsemane. Judas led the way. His final act of betrayal had come. Judas went right up to Jesus and kissed his cheek as a signal. The soldiers closed in. And so began a long, painful night of lies, sin, and misunderstanding.

On the walk to Golgotha, "the place of the skull," Jesus carried a heavy, wooden cross on his bleeding back. Each step was a painful struggle.

Then Roman soldiers nailed Jesus to the cross. And in a few hours, Jesus died. For you. For me. For the whole world.

In the greatest act of love we will ever know, Jesus took our sins away. He paid for them on the cross. And now, if we believe he is our Savior, we can live with him forever in heaven someday.

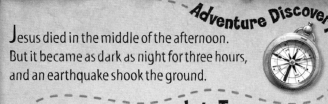

Adventure Discovery

Jesus died in the middle of the afternoon. But it became as dark as night for three hours, and an earthquake shook the ground.

Words to Treasure

But here is how God has shown his love for us. While we were still sinners, Christ died for us.

Romans 5:8

Jesus Is Alive!

Mark 16:1 – 11

The tomb was empty! How could it be? The huge stone had been rolled away from the entrance. Mary Magdalene, Salome, and Mary, the mother of James, had brought spices with them to put on Jesus' body.

But his body wasn't there!

When they walked inside the tomb, they saw an angel dressed in a white robe. "Don't be alarmed," he said. "You are looking for Jesus the Nazarene, who was crucified. But he has risen! He is not here!"

Then the angel said, "Go! Tell his disciples and Peter, 'Jesus is going ahead of you into Galilee. There you will see him. It will be just as he told you.'"

Adventure Discovery

The women brought spices to put on Jesus' body to show their love and affection for him.

Words to Treasure

"He has risen!"

Mark 16:6

Heaven Bound

Acts 1:1 – 11

After his suffering and death, Jesus appeared to his disciples for forty days. They were a little scared, surprised, and happy all at the same time. Jesus proved that he was alive again by eating with them and showing them scars from the nails in his hands.

While Jesus was with them, he continued to tell them about God's kingdom. One day he said, "Wait in Jerusalem for the gift my Father promised. You have heard me talk about it. John baptized with water. But in a few days you will be baptized with the Holy Spirit. Once you receive the power of the Holy Spirit, you will be my witnesses to the whole world by telling them about me."

Then as the disciples watched, Jesus was taken up to heaven. Soon a cloud hid Jesus from their sight.

Suddenly two men dressed in white clothes appeared next to the disciples. "Men of Galilee," they said, "why do you stand here looking at the sky? Jesus has been taken away into heaven. But he will come back."

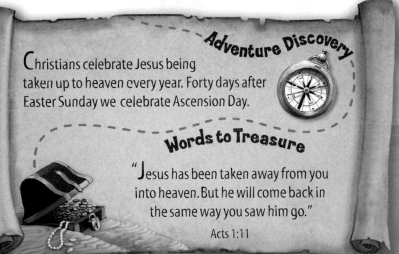

Adventure Discovery

Christians celebrate Jesus being taken up to heaven every year. Forty days after Easter Sunday we celebrate Ascension Day.

Words to Treasure

"Jesus has been taken away from you into heaven. But he will come back in the same way you saw him go."

Acts 1:11

Spirit Fire

Acts 2:1 – 41

The disciples gathered in a house in Jerusalem, like Jesus had told them to do before he was taken to heaven. Suddenly, surprisingly, a rushing, whirling wind started to blow *inside* the house!

Something that looked like tongues of fire settled on each person in the room. But it didn't burn them or hurt them. They were filled with the Holy Spirit and were given the power to speak in languages they had not known before.

Jewish people from every country in the world were staying in the city of Jerusalem. When they heard the men of Galilee speaking in their own languages, they were amazed and confused.

Peter explained to them that the Holy Spirit had come. It was just as the great prophet Joel had predicted. Peter quoted the Bible saying, "Everyone who calls out to me will be saved" (Joel 2:32).

Peter continued, "So be sure of this, all you people of Israel. You nailed Jesus to the cross. But God has made him both Lord and Christ."

When the people heard this, they felt ashamed. They asked Peter and the other apostles, "What should we do?"

Peter replied, "Turn away from your sins and be baptized in the name of Jesus Christ. Then your sins will be forgiven. You will receive the gift of the Holy Spirit."

About three thousand people joined the believers that day!

Adventure Discovery

The Holy Spirit is part of the Holy Trinity of God — the Father, the Son, and the Holy Spirit.

Words to Treasure

All of them were filled with the Holy Spirit.

Acts 2:4

Jail Quake

Acts 16:16 – 40

Paul and Silas weren't ordinary men. Even in the middle of the night while they sat in jail, they did an extraordinary thing — they prayed and sang songs to God. As other prisoners listened, their voices echoed against the cold stone walls. Their feet were in chains. They had been cruelly beaten and whipped. But still, they chose to praise and worship God.

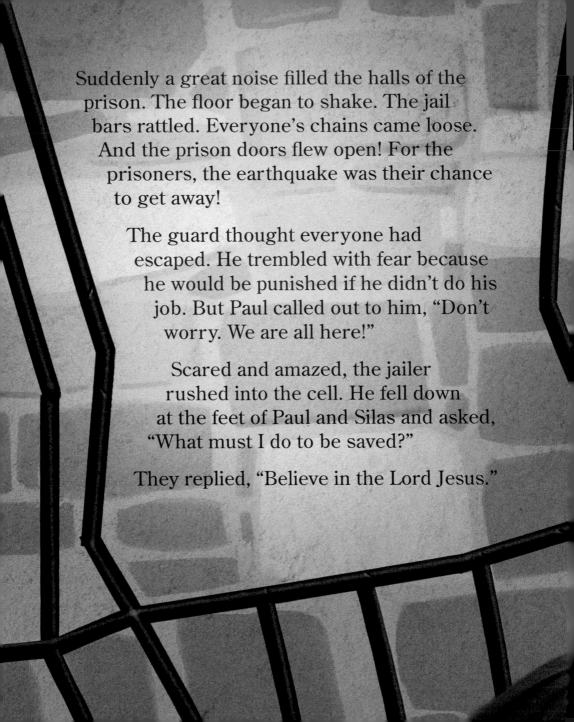

Suddenly a great noise filled the halls of the prison. The floor began to shake. The jail bars rattled. Everyone's chains came loose. And the prison doors flew open! For the prisoners, the earthquake was their chance to get away!

The guard thought everyone had escaped. He trembled with fear because he would be punished if he didn't do his job. But Paul called out to him, "Don't worry. We are all here!"

Scared and amazed, the jailer rushed into the cell. He fell down at the feet of Paul and Silas and asked, "What must I do to be saved?"

They replied, "Believe in the Lord Jesus."

The jailer took Paul and Silas to his house where he and his whole family were baptized. Their lives were changed forever, and they were filled with incredible joy.

The next morning, Paul and Silas were set free. They traveled to other places in order to tell more people about Jesus.

Adventure Discovery

Paul and Silas were punished and thrown into jail because they had helped a slave girl.

Words to Treasure

"Believe in the Lord Jesus. Then you and your family will be saved."

Acts 16:31

Shipwrecked!

Acts 27:13 — 28:10

Paul clung to a chunk of wood as he drifted ashore. The battered ship he had been sailing on crashed against the rocks near the Island of Malta. Thankful to be alive, Paul crawled onto the beach.

By God's mercy all 276 men survived the shipwreck. It was just as the angel had told Paul: "Do not be afraid, Paul … God has shown his grace by sparing the lives of all those sailing with you."

It was cold and raining, so the men made a campfire. As Paul added more sticks to the fire, a snake darted out and bit Paul's hand!

He flicked the deadly snake off his arm, but the native people watched and worried. How long until Paul started to swell up and suffer from the poison?

Miraculously Paul was fine. Nothing happened to him. The people were amazed.

During the three months that Paul stayed with the people of Malta, he healed them of their sicknesses and diseases. And he told them about Jesus and what it means to be a Christian.

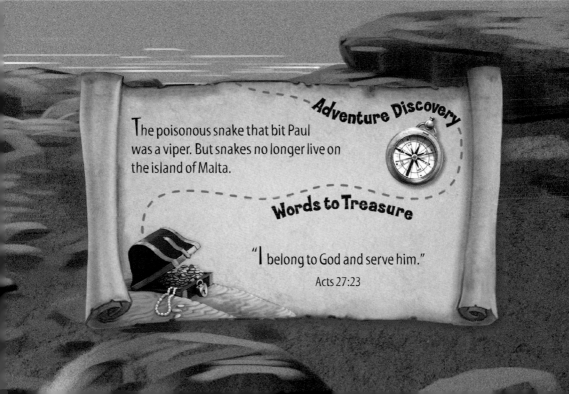

Adventure Discovery

The poisonous snake that bit Paul was a viper. But snakes no longer live on the island of Malta.

Words to Treasure

"I belong to God and serve him."

Acts 27:23

The Journeys of Paul

Rome

Paul traveled to many places.
Everywhere he went, he told
people about Jesus. He helped
spread the news of
Jesus our Savior
throughout the world.

Syracuse

Philippi

Thessalonica

Antioch

Lystra

Ephesus

Derbe

Athens

Attalia

Corinth

Tarsus

Salamis

Paphos

Antioch

Tyre

Caesarea

Jerusalem

The Adventure Continues...

So ends our journey through some of the stories in the New Testament. We've had many adventures along the way, from Jesus' birth to Paul and his work spreading the gospel around the world.

But the adventure isn't over. The most important thing has yet to happen ... Jesus is coming back!

Here are some clues from the Bible about Jesus' return to earth from heaven:

1 Thessalonians 4:1–17	Jesus will return someday to take his followers home.
Acts 1:11	Jesus will return the same way he left.
Luke 21:8	Many will pretend to be like Jesus and mislead a lot of people.
Revelation 20:10	Satan will be punished and defeated; Satan will not win, God will.
Luke 21:34 – 36	Jesus will come at a time when we do not expect. So we need to be ready.
Matthew 28:18 – 20	Jesus calls us to continue the work he started until he returns.
John 20:21	Again Jesus said, "May peace be with you! The Father has sent me. So now I am sending you."

Words to Treasure

But the Lord is faithful. He will strengthen you.
He will guard you from the evil one.

2 Thessalonians 3:3

Check out the entire Adventure Bible Family

A journey of faith begins with the first step. From preschoolers to pre-teens, the *Adventure Bible* helps kids find their way.

For Kids 6-9

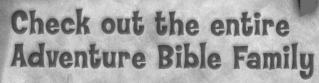

Designed especially for early readers who are ready to explore the Bible on their own.

9780310715474

This yearlong devotional takes children on a thrilling journey of spiritual growth and discovery.

9780310714484

NIrV Adventure BIBLE for Early Readers

365 Days of Adventure
NIrV Adventure BIBLE Book of Devotions for Early Readers

Written by Marnie Wooding

For Kids 9-12

Filled with great adventures and exciting features, this #1 Bible for kids opens a fresh new encounter with God's Word.

9780310715436

A full year's worth of daily devotions for kids that will capture their imagination, teach them about God, and help them live a life of faith.

9780310714477

Available at your local bookstore!